PRACTICING THE ART OF

gratitude

BY APPRECIATING THE LITTLE THINGS

this book belongs to

✉ Email us at FREEBIES @ JUNELUCY.COM
to get a FREE printable download!

FOR A LITTLE INSPIRATION
follow along at:

◎ @JUNEANDLUCY

f @JUNEANDLUCY

WWW. JUNELUCY.COM

Shop our other books at
www.junelucy.com

Wholesale distribution through Ingram Content Group
www.ingramcontent.com/publishers/distribution/wholesale

For questions and customer service, email us at
support@junelucy.com

DID YOU GO ALL DAY WITHOUT SPILLING COFFEE ALL OVER YOURSELF?
WAS THERE ENOUGH TOILET PAPER IN THE BATHROOM?
DID YOUR CHILD GO AN ENTIRE DAY WITHOUT EATING CRAYONS?
WAS THERE ENOUGH CLEAN LAUNDRY TO LAST THE WHOLE DAY?
DID YOU GO ALL DAY WITHOUT STEPPING ON A LEGO?
DID YOU GET TO WEAR YOGA PANTS ALL DAY?
WERE YOU ABLE TO GET ALL THE WAY TO WORK WITHOUT RUNNING OUT OF GAS?
DID YOU WAKE UP BEFORE YOUR ALARM?
WERE YOU ABLE TO BUY SOMETHING WITH EXACT CHANGE?
DID YOU FIND MONEY IN THE POCKET OF AN OLD PAIR OF PANTS?
WAS YOUR AVOCADO PERFECTLY RIPE?

PRACTICING THE ART OF
gratitude
BY APPRECIATING THE LITTLE THINGS

We often find ourselves waiting for the big things in life to happen before we consider ourselves lucky and express our gratitude. We wait for the big promotion, the pay raise, an engagement, or some other huge life event to reflect on how grateful we are for our good fortune. But what about the beautiful and amazing little things that make up each and every day in between? It may be something funny that happened to you, or something unexpected that put a smile on your face. Maybe it was something completely ordinary that you have never taken the time to reflect on and truly appreciate. Our lives are beautiful as a result of thousands of little moments in between the big life events.

Try to capture 2 or 3 of these little moments each week (don't stress over capturing a moment each day!) and you may just be surprised as you look back and realize each of those little things were actually the big things.

There is ALWAYS Something to be GRATEFUL for

A LITTLE THING

AN ORDINARY THING

A FUNNY THING

A WEIRD THING

AN UNEXPECTED THING

A KIND THING

There is ALWAYS Something to be GRATEFUL for

A LITTLE THING

AN ORDINARY THING

A FUNNY THING

A WEIRD THING

AN UNEXPECTED THING

A KIND THING

There is ALWAYS something to be GRATEFUL for

A LITTLE THING

AN ORDINARY THING

A FUNNY THING

A WEIRD THING

AN UNEXPECTED THING

A KIND THING

THERE IS ALWAYS SOMETHING TO BE GRATEFUL FOR

A LITTLE THING

AN ORDINARY THING

A FUNNY THING

_____
_____
_____
_____
_____
_____

A WEIRD THING

_____
_____
_____
_____
_____
_____
_____
_____

AN UNEXPECTED THING

_____
_____
_____
_____
_____
_____
_____

A KIND THING

There is ALWAYS Something TO BE GRATEFUL for

A LITTLE THING

AN ORDINARY THING

A FUNNY THING

Very LITTLE is NEEDED to make a HAPPY life; it is all within YOURSELF in your way of thinking.

— MARCUS AURELIUS

There is ALWAYS something TO BE GRATEFUL for

A LITTLE THING

AN ORDINARY THING

A FUNNY THING

A WEIRD THING

AN UNEXPECTED THING

A KIND THING

A LITTLE THING

AN ORDINARY THING

A FUNNY THING

A WEIRD THING

AN UNEXPECTED THING

A KIND THING

A LITTLE THING

AN ORDINARY THING

A FUNNY THING

A WEIRD THING

AN UNEXPECTED THING

A KIND THING

There is ALWAYS Something TO BE GRATEFUL for

A LITTLE THING

AN ORDINARY THING

A FUNNY THING

A WEIRD THING

AN UNEXPECTED THING

A KIND THING

There is ALWAYS Something to be GRATEFUL for

/ /

A LITTLE THING

/ /

AN ORDINARY THING

/ /

A FUNNY THING

A WEIRD THING

AN UNEXPECTED THING

A KIND THING

There is ALWAYS something to be GRATEFUL for

A LITTLE THING

AN ORDINARY THING

A FUNNY THING

A WEIRD THING

AN UNEXPECTED THING

A KIND THING

things turn out BEST for people who make the BEST of the way things turn out.

– JOHN WOODEN

A WEIRD THING

AN UNEXPECTED THING

A KIND THING

THERE IS ALWAYS SOMETHING TO BE GRATEFUL FOR

_____ / /

A LITTLE THING

_____ / /

AN ORDINARY THING

_____ / /

A FUNNY THING

A WEIRD THING

AN UNEXPECTED THING

A KIND THING

There is ALWAYS Something TO BE GRATEFUL for

A LITTLE THING

AN ORDINARY THING

A FUNNY THING

A WEIRD THING

AN UNEXPECTED THING

A KIND THING

A LITTLE THING

AN ORDINARY THING

A FUNNY THING

_____

A WEIRD THING

_____

AN UNEXPECTED THING

_____

A KIND THING

There is ALWAYS something to be GRATEFUL for

A LITTLE THING

AN ORDINARY THING

A FUNNY THING

A WEIRD THING

AN UNEXPECTED THING

A KIND THING

THERE IS ALWAYS SOMETHING TO BE GRATEFUL FOR

A LITTLE THING

AN ORDINARY THING

A FUNNY THING

A WEIRD THING

AN UNEXPECTED THING

A KIND THING

A LITTLE THING

AN ORDINARY THING

A FUNNY THING

enjoy the little
THINGS,
for one day you
may look back
AND realize they
were the BIG
things.

— ROBERT BRAULT

There is ALWAYS Something to be GRATEFUL for

_____ / /

A LITTLE THING

_____ / /

AN ORDINARY THING

_____ / /

A FUNNY THING

A WEIRD THING

AN UNEXPECTED THING

A KIND THING

There is ALWAYS something to be GRATEFUL for

A LITTLE THING

AN ORDINARY THING

A FUNNY THING

A WEIRD THING

AN UNEXPECTED THING

A KIND THING

There is ALWAYS something TO BE GRATEFUL for

A LITTLE THING

AN ORDINARY THING

A FUNNY THING

A WEIRD THING

AN UNEXPECTED THING

A KIND THING

There is ALWAYS something to be grateful for

A LITTLE THING

AN ORDINARY THING

A FUNNY THING

A WEIRD THING

AN UNEXPECTED THING

A KIND THING

There is ALWAYS something to be GRATEFUL for

A LITTLE THING _____ / /

AN ORDINARY THING

A FUNNY THING _____ / /

A WEIRD THING

AN UNEXPECTED THING

A KIND THING

A LITTLE THING

AN ORDINARY THING

A FUNNY THING

A WEIRD THING

AN UNEXPECTED THING

A KIND THING

it is not JOY that makes us GRATEFUL. it is gratitude THAT makes us JOYFUL.

— DAVID STEINDL-RAST

A WEIRD THING

AN UNEXPECTED THING

A KIND THING

There is ALWAYS something to be GRATEFUL for

A LITTLE THING

AN ORDINARY THING

A FUNNY THING

A WEIRD THING

AN UNEXPECTED THING

A KIND THING

There is ALWAYS something TO BE GRATEFUL for

A LITTLE THING

AN ORDINARY THING

A FUNNY THING

A WEIRD THING

AN UNEXPECTED THING

A KIND THING

There is ALWAYS something TO BE GRATEFUL for

A LITTLE THING

AN ORDINARY THING

A FUNNY THING

A WEIRD THING

AN UNEXPECTED THING

A KIND THING

There is ALWAYS something to be grateful for

A LITTLE THING

AN ORDINARY THING

A FUNNY THING

_____

A WEIRD THING

_____

AN UNEXPECTED THING

_____

A KIND THING

There is ALWAYS something to be GRATEFUL for

A LITTLE THING

AN ORDINARY THING

A FUNNY THING

A WEIRD THING

AN UNEXPECTED THING

A KIND THING

There is ALWAYS something TO BE GRATEFUL for

/ /

A LITTLE THING

/ /

AN ORDINARY THING

/ /

A FUNNY THING

gratitude TURNS what we have into ENOUGH.

– MELODY BEATTIE

A LITTLE THING

AN ORDINARY THING

A FUNNY THING

A WEIRD THING

AN UNEXPECTED THING

A KIND THING

A LITTLE THING

AN ORDINARY THING

A FUNNY THING

A WEIRD THING

AN UNEXPECTED THING

A KIND THING

There is ALWAYS something to be GRATEFUL for

A LITTLE THING

AN ORDINARY THING

A FUNNY THING

A WEIRD THING

AN UNEXPECTED THING

A KIND THING

There is ALWAYS something to be GRATEFUL for

A LITTLE THING

AN ORDINARY THING

A FUNNY THING

A WEIRD THING

AN UNEXPECTED THING

A KIND THING

There is ALWAYS something TO BE GRATEFUL for

//

A LITTLE THING

//

AN ORDINARY THING

//

A FUNNY THING

A WEIRD THING

AN UNEXPECTED THING

A KIND THING

THERE IS ALWAYS SOMETHING TO BE GRATEFUL FOR

A LITTLE THING

AN ORDINARY THING

A FUNNY THING

A WEIRD THING

AN UNEXPECTED THING

A KIND THING

no matter what the situation is... close your EYES and think of all the THINGS in your life you COULD be grateful for right NOW.

— DEEPAK CHOPRA

A WEIRD THING

AN UNEXPECTED THING

A KIND THING

There is ALWAYS something to be GRATEFUL for

A LITTLE THING

AN ORDINARY THING

A FUNNY THING

A WEIRD THING

AN UNEXPECTED THING

A KIND THING

There is ALWAYS Something to be GRATEFUL for

A LITTLE THING

AN ORDINARY THING

A FUNNY THING

A WEIRD THING

AN UNEXPECTED THING

A KIND THING

THERE IS ALWAYS SOMETHING TO BE GRATEFUL FOR

_____ / / _____

A LITTLE THING

_____ / / _____

AN ORDINARY THING

_____ / / _____

A FUNNY THING

A WEIRD THING

AN UNEXPECTED THING

A KIND THING

There is ALWAYS Something TO BE GRATEFUL for

A LITTLE THING

AN ORDINARY THING

A FUNNY THING

A WEIRD THING

AN UNEXPECTED THING

A KIND THING

There is ALWAYS something to be GRATEFUL for

A LITTLE THING

AN ORDINARY THING

A FUNNY THING

A WEIRD THING

AN UNEXPECTED THING

A KIND THING

THERE IS ALWAYS SOMETHING TO BE GRATEFUL FOR

___ / ___ / ___

A LITTLE THING

___ / ___ / ___

AN ORDINARY THING

___ / ___ / ___

A FUNNY THING

never let
the things you
WANT make
you forget the
THINGS
you have.

There is ALWAYS something to be GRATEFUL for

A LITTLE THING

AN ORDINARY THING

A FUNNY THING

A WEIRD THING

AN UNEXPECTED THING

A KIND THING

THERE IS ALWAYS SOMETHING TO BE GRATEFUL FOR

A LITTLE THING

AN ORDINARY THING

A FUNNY THING

A WEIRD THING

AN UNEXPECTED THING

A KIND THING

There is ALWAYS something to be GRATEFUL for

A LITTLE THING

AN ORDINARY THING

A FUNNY THING

A WEIRD THING

AN UNEXPECTED THING

A KIND THING

There is ALWAYS something TO BE GRATEFUL for

A LITTLE THING

AN ORDINARY THING

A FUNNY THING

A WEIRD THING

AN UNEXPECTED THING

A KIND THING

There is ALWAYS something to be GRATEFUL for

A LITTLE THING

AN ORDINARY THING

A FUNNY THING

A WEIRD THING

AN UNEXPECTED THING

A KIND THING

A LITTLE THING

AN ORDINARY THING

A FUNNY THING

A WEIRD THING

AN UNEXPECTED THING

A KIND THING

it is the
SWEET,
simple things
in life which
are the real ones
AFTERALL.

— LAURA INGALLS WILDER

A WEIRD THING

AN UNEXPECTED THING

A KIND THING

THERE IS ALWAYS SOMETHING TO BE GRATEFUL FOR

A LITTLE THING

AN ORDINARY THING

A FUNNY THING

A WEIRD THING

AN UNEXPECTED THING

A KIND THING

A LITTLE THING

AN ORDINARY THING

A FUNNY THING

A WEIRD THING

AN UNEXPECTED THING

A KIND THING

THERE IS ALWAYS something TO BE GRATEFUL FOR

A LITTLE THING

AN ORDINARY THING

A FUNNY THING

A WEIRD THING

AN UNEXPECTED THING

A KIND THING

THERE IS ALWAYS SOMETHING TO BE GRATEFUL FOR

A LITTLE THING

AN ORDINARY THING

A FUNNY THING

A WEIRD THING

AN UNEXPECTED THING

A KIND THING

There is ALWAYS something to be GRATEFUL for

A LITTLE THING

AN ORDINARY THING

A FUNNY THING

_____
_____
_____
_____
_____
_____
_____

A WEIRD THING

_____
_____
_____
_____
_____
_____
_____
_____
_____
_____

AN UNEXPECTED THING

_____
_____
_____
_____
_____
_____
_____
_____
_____

A KIND THING

THERE IS ALWAYS SOMETHING TO BE GRATEFUL FOR

A LITTLE THING

AN ORDINARY THING

A FUNNY THING

A WEIRD THING

AN UNEXPECTED THING

A KIND THING

There is ALWAYS something TO BE GRATEFUL for

A LITTLE THING

AN ORDINARY THING

A FUNNY THING

A WEIRD THING

AN UNEXPECTED THING

A KIND THING

There is ALWAYS something TO BE GRATEFUL for

A LITTLE THING

AN ORDINARY THING

A FUNNY THING

Made in the USA
Middletown, DE
12 December 2019